Miller 400

by Eric Ethan

Gareth Stevens Publishing
MILWAUKEE

The author wishes to thank Glen Fitzgerald, George Philips, Mary Jo Lindahl, and Juanita Jones for their help and encouragement.

For a free color catalog describing Gareth Stevens Publishing's list of high-quality books and multimedia programs, call 1-800-542-2595 (USA) or 1-800-461-9120 (Canada). Gareth Stevens Publishing's Fax: (414) 225-0377.

Library of Congress Cataloging-in-Publication Data

Ethan, Eric.
    Miller 400 / by Eric Ethan.
      p. cm. — (NASCAR! an imagination library series)
    Includes index.
    Summary: Describes the Miller 400, the first race sanctioned by the National Association for Stock Car Auto Racing (NASCAR) in 1969 and held annually at the Michigan Speedway in Brooklyn, Michigan.
    ISBN 0-8368-2139-4 (lib. bdg.)
    1. Miller 400 (Automobile race)—Juvenile literature. [1. Miller 400 (Automobile race). 2. Stock car racing.] I. Title. II. Series: Ethan, Eric. NASCAR! an imagination library series.
GV1033.5.M55E85   1999
796.72'06'877428—dc21   99-14633

First published in North America in 1999 by
Gareth Stevens Publishing
1555 North RiverCenter Drive, Suite 201
Milwaukee, WI 53212 USA

This edition © 1999 by Gareth Stevens, Inc. Text by Eric Ethan. Photographs © 1998: Cover, pp. 7, 13, 17, 19, 21 - Don Grassman; pp. 5, 11, 15 - Ernest Masche; Illustration: p. 9 - The Official NASCAR Preview and Press Guide. Additional end matter © 1999 by Gareth Stevens, Inc.

Text: Eric Ethan
Page layout: Lesley M. White
Cover design: Lesley M. White
Editorial assistant: Diane Laska

Printed in the United States of America

1 2 3 4 5 6 7 8 9 03 02 01 00 99

TABLE OF CONTENTS

The Miller 400 4

Michigan Speedway 6

The Track 8

NASCAR Racers 10

Mark Martin, Winner 14

Qualifying 16

The Race 18

Pit Action 20

Accidents and Safety 22

Glossary 23

Places to Write 23

Web Sites 24

Index 24

Metric Chart
1 mile = 1.609 kilometers
100 miles = 160.9 km
400 miles = 643.6 km

Words that appear in the glossary are printed in
boldface type the first time they occur in the text.

THE MILLER 400

The Miller 400 was first **sanctioned** by NASCAR — The National Association for **Stock Car** Auto Racing — in 1969. In that year, Cale Yarborough won the first race driving a 1969 Mercury **sedan**. He averaged 135 miles per hour during the race. Yarborough went on to win the Miller 400 six times, more than any other NASCAR driver.

The 400-mile race currently takes top drivers about 2½ hours to finish. It took Yarborough almost three hours — racing speeds were much slower in the early years. In 1996, driver Rusty Wallace set a new average-speed record for the race at 166.033 miles per hour.

The Michigan Speedway in Brooklyn, Michigan, is home to the Miller 400.
CIA Stock Photo: Ernest Masche

MICHIGAN SPEEDWAY

The Miller 400 takes place the second weekend in June each year at the Michigan Speedway in Brooklyn, Michigan. Brooklyn is located seventy miles southwest of Michigan's largest city, Detroit. Starting in 1999, the 400-mile race will be known as the Kmart 400 — sponsored by Kmart.

The Michigan Speedway is a large oval, two miles long. The turns are steeply **banked** toward the inside of the course. Charles Moneypenny and Sterling Moss designed the course, which was built in 1967. Moneypenny also designed the oval track at Daytona International Speedway in Florida. Moss is a world-famous driver who learned how to make racetracks safer and faster while racing on them around the world.

Steep banks, like the ones at the Michigan Speedway, help race cars go around the course faster without flying off the track.
CIA Stock Photo: Don Grassman

THE TRACK

Michigan Speedway's design makes it a very popular track with race fans. It has a very wide racing surface. This allows three or four cars to race next to each other all around the track. Side-by-side competition at high speed adds excitement to a race.

Each year, over ninety thousand fans attend the Miller 400, and many more watch it at home on television. When Moneypenny and Sterling planned their design, they made sure spectators could see the entire track from nearly every seat.

The large, oval track at the Michigan Speedway has a small bend in front of the center grandstand.
The Official NASCAR Preview and Press Guide

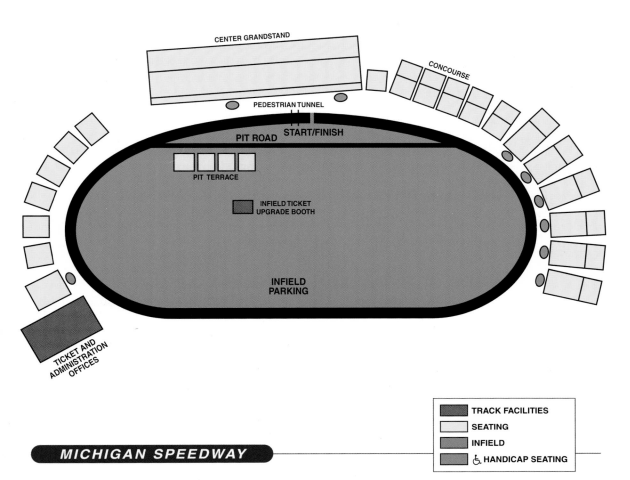

CENTER GRANDSTAND

CONCOURSE

PEDESTRIAN TUNNEL

START/FINISH

PIT ROAD

PIT TERRACE

INFIELD TICKET UPGRADE BOOTH

INFIELD PARKING

TICKET AND ADMINISTRATION OFFICES

	TRACK FACILITIES
	SEATING
	INFIELD
♿	HANDICAP SEATING

MICHIGAN SPEEDWAY

Distance: *2 Miles*

Banking: *18 degrees*

Qualifying Record: *Jeff Gordon, 186.611 mph (38.5883 seconds), set June 16, 1995*

Race Record (400 Miles): *Rusty Wallace, 166.033 mph, set June 23, 1996*

NASCAR RACERS

NASCAR racers may look a little like the family car sitting in the driveway. The only parts they have in common, however, are the hood, roof, and trunk lid. Everything else is specially built from the ground up according to NASCAR rules. Most racing teams buy the frame, or **chassis**, from an outside source. Then they add the **suspension**, tires, interior, and body panels. Motors are built by hand. Every NASCAR racing team has to follow the same rules.

Building one or more cars by hand from parts is very expensive, so teams are sponsored by various companies. The companies pay money to the NASCAR teams in exchange for the placement of advertising **logos** on the car.

Driver Kyle Petty's car is covered with logos.
CIA Stock Photo: Ernest Masche

11

NASCAR racers have a very **aerodynamic** design. This means they create as little wind resistance as possible when moving around the track at high speed. The lower the car is to the ground, the lower the wind resistance and the faster the car. NASCAR has rules to limit how low a car can be. This is for safety reasons. Another part of the frame is the roll cage that protects the driver.

NASCAR also requires race cars to use cast-iron motors. Cast iron is very strong and cools quickly. It can take the stress and heat that NASCAR racing creates.

Dale Jarrett leads Bill Elliott and Jeff Burton late in the 1998 running of the Miller 400.
CIA Stock Photo: Don Grassman

MARK MARTIN, WINNER

Mark Martin won the 1998 Miller 400. He drove car number six sponsored by the Valvoline Motor Oil Company. Car number six looks like a Ford Thunderbird. The owner is Jack Roush of Roush Racing.

Martin has driven in NASCAR races since 1981. He had won over $18 million and finished first twenty-nine times at the end of the 1998 season.

Mark Martin's winning car speeds through a tight corner during the Miller 400.
CIA Stock Photo: Ernest Masche

QUALIFYING

In the days before the actual race, drivers get a chance to learn the track, and team mechanics make their final adjustments. Each track is different, so cars need to be tuned to each track.

Racing teams have more than one available engine. They use one engine just for **qualifying**. It is adjusted to produce all-out power to set the fastest possible lap time. It is then replaced by a second engine for race day. Burning out an engine during qualifying can be worth it. Qualifying speeds decide the starting order of the cars in the race.

Although a race-day engine is tuned for power, achieving good gas mileage and having a strong cooling system are also important to make sure a car survives the entire race.

Jeff Gordon and race-winner Mark Martin pass the main grandstand during the 1998 Miller 400.
CIA Stock Photo: Don Grassman

THE RACE

When the **starter** drops the green flag, each driver speeds off. Drivers immediately look for the groove in the track. Every track has a groove, or the best path to take on the straightaways and corners. Finding the groove means going faster while using less gasoline. The groove is sometimes visible as a dark line on a lighter racing surface. Tire rubber, exhaust, and oil build up to make the groove.

Once drivers find the groove, their goal is to survive the race going as fast as possible, while avoiding accidents and conserving gasoline. They push their cars as hard as they can without damaging them. Breakdowns and running out of gas put more cars out of races than accidents.

Jeff Gordon leads a pack of cars coming into the corner at the 1998 Miller 400.
CIA Stock Photo: Don Grassman

PIT ACTION

One of the ways drivers conserve fuel and give their engines a rest is called **drafting**. This means a car gets very close to another car just ahead of it. The first car pushes air out of the way for the second car. The second car goes just as fast as the first, but its engine doesn't have to work as hard or use as much fuel as the one in front.

When a race car needs new tires or fuel, it heads into the pit. A highly trained pit crew changes the tires and fills the fuel tank in the fastest time possible. Pit stops can cost a race car its position on the track. The winning drivers usually have the best pit crews. In 1996, when Rusty Wallace won the Miller 400, his pit crew triumphed over thirty-five other pit crews to win the Pit Crew Strategy Award.

A pit crew works quickly to change tires and refuel during the 1998 Miller 400.
CIA Stock Photo: Don Grassman

ACCIDENTS AND SAFETY

Every race car driver accepts accidents as a risk of racing. Mechanics, track designers, and drivers do everything they can to make the sport safe. The weight of a car slows it down, so each team wants its car to weigh what the rules require, but no more. Even though materials used in the cars are lightweight, they are very strong. Steel tube frames and roll cages absorb a lot of force. Drivers have walked away from terrible accidents thanks to modern safety design and materials.

Flying metal and other parts of a car can be a danger to the crowd. A banked track, elevated seating, retaining walls, and impact-absorbing fences help keep cars on the track.

GLOSSARY

You can find these words on the pages listed. Reading a word in a sentence helps you understand it even better.

aerodynamic (AIR-oh-die-NAM-ick) — shaped so air flows around it easily when it moves 12

banked — inclined upward from the inside edge 6

chassis (CHAS-ee) — the frame and working parts of a car 10

drafting (DRAF-ting) — when one car follows closely behind another 20

logos (LOW-gos) — graphic designs that feature a company name/product 10

qualifying (KWAH-lih-fy-ing) — a test that makes a person or object fit for a certain position 16

sanctioned (SANK-shunned) — an object, idea, or event that is approved by an official group 4

sedan (seh-DAN) — a car with two or four doors and both front and rear seats 4

starter — a person who signals the beginning of a race 18

stock car — a new-model sedan manufactured by Detroit automakers, such as Ford, General Motors, and Chevrolet 4

suspension (sus-PEN-shun) — a system of devices that supports the upper part of a vehicle on its axles 10

PLACES TO WRITE

International Motor Sports Museum
Public Relations Manager
3198 Speedway Boulevard
Talladega, AL 35160

Daytona USA
Public Relations Manager
1801 West International Boulevard
Daytona Beach, FL 32114

Motorbooks International
Public Relations Manager
729 Prospect Avenue/Box 1
Osceola, WI 54020

Michigan Speedway — *host to the Kmart 400 (formerly the Miller 400)*
12626 U.S. 12
Brooklyn, MI 49230

WEB SITES

www.nascar.com

This is the official web site of the National Association for Stock Car Auto Racing.

www.ciastockphoto.com

This is one of the best NASCAR photo sites. It is the source of many of the pictures in this book. It presents new images during each racing season.

racing.yahoo.com/rac/nascar

At this web site, race fans can find current NASCAR race results, standings, schedules, driver profiles, feature stories, and merchandise.

Due to the dynamic nature of the Internet, some web sites stay current longer than others. To find additional web sites, use a reliable search engine with one or more of the following keywords: *Mark Martin, Michigan Speedway, Miller 400, Sterling Moss, NASCAR, Jack Roush, Roush Racing, Rusty Wallace,* and *Cale Yarborough.*

INDEX

accidents 18, 22
aerodynamic design 12

banked track 6-7
Brooklyn, Michigan 4, 6

chassis 10

drafting 20
drivers 4, 6, 10-11, 12, 16, 18, 20, 22

fans 8
frames 10
fuel 12, 16, 18, 20-21, 22

logos 10-11

Martin, Mark 14-15, 16-17
mechanics 16, 22
Mercury 4
Michigan Speedway 4-5, 6-7, 8-9
Moneypenny, Charles 6, 8
Moss, Sterling 6, 8

NASCAR 4, 10, 12, 14

oval 6, 8

pit crews 20-21

pits 20

qualifying 9, 16

Roush, Jack 14

sedans 4
sponsors 10

tires 10, 18, 20-21
track 6-7, 8-9, 12, 16, 18, 20, 22

Wallace, Rusty 4, 20

Yarborough, Cale 4